Cremation and the Bible

The Burning Of Human Bodies To Ashes

Cremation and the Bible
The Burning Of Human Bodies To Ashes

Published by
Into Thine Hand
4141 NW 39th Ave
Fort Lauderdale FL 33309
www.intothinehand.com

ISBN: 978-0-9841231-6-2

All Scripture quotations are taken from the Holy Bible, King James
Version, Copyright © 1977, 1984, Thomas Nelson Inc., Publishers.

Table of Contents

Cremation Introduced

From what sector or region of human existence has cremation originated and what was the original purpose of the
practice of cremation? Has this practice emerged from a
religious, cultural, civil, paranormal origin or otherwise?

What percentage of the population of our world, more
strikingly, our immediate regions would consider, are considering or have already determined that cremation is their
disposal of choice for theirs or their family's remains?
What factors serve to influence the inclination or conclu-
sion towards the option of cremation of one's remains as
a choice?

Most importantly, what would you factor in for yourself
and or family members as the reasons why you would consider or have considered cremation as an option to dispose
of yours or their remains? Or is that even an option for
you and your family, if not why not?

Do you believe that education or the lack thereof is a key
factor in one embracing or not embracing the choice of
cremationas an option for theirs or their family's remains? Do you believe that most of the people who em-
brace the option of cremation have adequate knowledge of
the pros and the cons, the origin and the original purpose
of that option or to the contrary? More personally, how
much do you know about the subject of cremation?

If you had a chance to witness the actual process of the
burning of the body, do you believe that you would remain
the same in your selection of the disposal of one's remains? Most importantly, would you remain the same in
your selection of the disposal of yours or your loved ones
remains?

The Burning of Human Bodies to Ashes

According to one source, Cremation rates vary widely across the world with some countries like Japan, Nepal and Thailand having a rate over 95% while other countries like Italy, Ireland and Poland having less than 10%. Factors include culture and religion; for example, the cremation rate in Muslim, Eastern Orthodox, and Roman Catholic majority countries is much lower due to religious sanctions on cremation whereas for Hindu or Buddhist majority countries the cremation rate is much higher. https://en.wikipedia.org/wiki/List_of_countries_by_crema tion_rate

However, the questions that are most important to you are how much do you know about the subject of cremation? What are the pros and the cons plus the origin and the original purpose of the practice of cremation?

This work is about providing a comprehensive biblical as well as some secular knowledge regarding the subject of cremation. It is about exegeting the origin and the original purpose of the practice of cremation down through biblical history. It is also about helping you to determine if this is a viable option for believers, especially, and also for humanity at large.

Chapter 1
What is Cremation?

Cremation is the process of reducing bodies to basic chemical compounds such as gasses and bone fragments. This is accomplished through high-temperature burning, vaporization and oxidation.[1] Cremation may serve as a funeral or post-funeral rite that is an alternative to the interment of an intact body in a casket. Cremated remains, which do not constitute a health risk, may be buried or interred in memorial sites or cemeteries, or they may be legally retained by relatives and dispersed in a variety of ways.

In many countries, cremation is usually done in a crematorium, but other countries prefer different methods. An example is the common crematorium) practice of open-air cremation in India and in Nepal.
— http://en.wikipedia.org/wiki/Cremation —

God has classified the act of cremation as a transgression This means that it is a deviation from the biblical standards, the standard of God and as such is a sin.

First, let's examine what God through the prophet Amos has to say about this practice. *[Amos 2:1] Thus saith the Lord; For three **transgressions** of Moab and for four, I will not*

The Burning of Human Bodies to Ashes

*turn away the punishment thereof; because **he burned the bones of the king of Edom into lime:***

The Moabites were so cruel against the King of Edom, that they burnt his bones after he was dead: which declared their barbarous rage, that they would avenge themselves upon the dead. – *Geneva Study Bible* –

The instance given refers not to the people of God, but to a heathen like themselves: The king of Moab burnt the bones of the king of Edom into lime. – *Matthew Henry's Commentory* –

This passage teaches us that regardless of our reasons for considering cremation, or who we are, believers or unbelievers, the act of cremation is a sin in the sight of God.

Though this act of cremation was done out of revenge and as a punishment to the king of Edom, that is not a method of the disposal of the human body that God subscribes to or permit humanity to either. Notice that God did not say that He was going to punish them because of the motive, but because of the act... because *they burned the bones into lime*

The writer of the book of second Kings classified cremation as a symbol of spiritual defilement or pollution. Notice what he says about the practice of cremation. *[2 Kings 23:16] And as Josiah turned himself, he spied the sepulchres that were there in the mount, and sent, and took the bones out of the sepulchres, and burned them upon the altar, and polluted it, according to the word of the Lord which the man of God proclaimed, who proclaimed these words. [2 Kings 23:9-10] 9. Nevertheless the priests of the high places came not up to the altar of the Lord in Jerusalem, but they did eat of the unleavened bread among their brethren. 10. And he defiled Topheth, which is in the valley of the children of Hinnom, that no man might make his son or his daughter to pass through the fire to Molech.*

Notice that based on *[2 Kings 23:16]* by burning the bones of the human carcass on the altar, that constituted the pollution or defilement of the altar.

Notice further that this classification of pollution or defilement was the word of the Lord.

Based on *[2 Kings 23:10]* the very place **Topheth** where the practice of cremation took place was in a state of defilement because the act was done there.

The latter part of *[2 Kings 23:10]* confirms that the children of Israel were given a clear commandment that they should not make their son and daughter pass through the fire

Let's note here that the passing through the fire did not mean that the son came out on the other side of the fire. He never came back out. He was consumed and burned to ashes in the midst of the fire.

There is a form of cremation that is called live cremation where the living person is burned to ashes in sacrifice unto idols. This practice was originated and perpetuated by the heathens not by the people or God.

The writer of the book of second kinds weighed in on this again. *[2 Kings 21:6]* *And **he made his son pass through the fire** and observed times, and used enchantments, and **dealt with familiar spirits and wizards**: he wrought **much wickedness in the sight of the Lord**, to provoke him to anger.*

Here we are faced with a Jewish king trying to adopt the pagan practice of what I would classify as live cremation This act was a pagan practice of offering up their sons or daughters to their gods in the most inhumane way.

Notice that in the process, he had to deal with familiar spirit or demons and wizards or witches the seat of where this practice is rooted. The people of God adopting the pagan practiceof offering up their children as sacrifices unto strange gods. This sacrifice was certainly not offered unto Jehovah God because He neither requested that of them nor would he accept such offering.

The question arises regarding the request that God made of Abraham to offer up his son Isaac on the alter as a sacrifice unto Him. Let's note that this was not the norm but a single exception because it was a type unto God the Father who would offer up his only Son on the cross of Calvary unto Himself. This was never done prior to this, neither has it been done there after. This is because this was pointing to the one act of sacrifice of God's Son, Jesus Christ who would be offered up as a sacrifice on the cross off Calvary. Notice further, that God stopped Abraham and stated that He, that is God, would provide Himself a lamb This meant that He, Himself, in the form of His Son, would become the lamb for the sins of the world.

Notice also that this act along with the other evil acts that this king had committed was classified as much wickedness in the sight of the Lord.

Notice further that this practice was considered one that provoked God to anger. There is no way that this could be approved by God and anger Him at the same time. It is either one or the other and the Scripture say that it angered God.

The writer of Leviticus confirms that this act was a ritual done by pagans unto their pagan gods *[Liv. 18:21] And thou shalt not let any of thy seed pass through the fire to Molech neither shalt thou profane the name of thy God: I am the LORD. [Jer. 7:30-31] 30. For the children of Judah* *have done evil in my sight, saith the Lord: they have set their abominations in the house which is called by my name, to pollute it. 31. And they have built the high places of Tophet, which is in the valley of the son of Hinnom, to burn their sons and their daughters in the fire, which I com manded them not,* *neither came it into my heart.*

Molech was the god of the Ammonites and Phoenicians to whom some Israelites sacrificed their infants in the valley of Hinnom.

Notice further that not only the burning of the dead human carcass was against the biblical standards which are the stan - dards of God as brought out in *Amos 2:1 "...he burned the bones of the king f Edom into lime,"* but the burning of the live person also is, and quite likely, more gross.

Notice also that this was done unto Molech, the pagan god According to *[Jer. 7:30-31]* this practice was considered *evil in the sight of the Lord.* Observe: *And they have built the high places of Tophet, which is in the valley of the son of Hinnom, to burn their sons and their daughters in the fire, which I commanded them not, neither came it into my heart.*

Passing through the fire is not as it sounds, because **the per- son who entered the fire did not come back out... he was consumed by the fire and burned to ashes.**

Based on the latter part of *[Jer. 7:31]* it is clear that the act of making their children pass through the fire was **actually burning them in the fire** "... *to burn their sons and their daughters in the fire"*

This is what is **considered child sacrifice, where they of- fered their child as a sacrifice unto their gods.** This is one of the worst form of child sacrifice, because the tone of the passage indicates that the child is the one who actually

12

walked into the fire

It is the writer's belief that it isn't impossible and highly probable that just as *the Muslim extremist train their children to volunteer for a suicide mission as martyrdom and they will have seventy two virgins in paradise, the children of the pagans who practiced child sacrifice, conditioned their children to volunteer to walk through the fire as a gift to their gods.*

This act is done today in some quarters during Halloween as a devil's sacrifice.. *see Satanists plot child sacrifice – internet article*

Satanists plot child sacrifice By Jim Cairns Kilkenny Ireland
Former link: ~~http://www.missingpersons-ireland.freepress-freespeech.com/archive_satanicchildsacrifice.htm~~ Warning!explicit material, not suited for children! The former link had the figures displayed below. Current link: http://www.hiddenmysteries.org/news/europe/ireland/101600a.html

Figure 1. Irish News of the World May 26th 1996 declares

that satanists plan to sacrifice a baby.The Labour TD , at that time , Mr John Mulvihill is seen in the lower image and he took this story very seriously at that time . I personally contacted John Mulvihill at that time after I was shown this article by none other than Born Again Christian , Dick Moore of Bagenalstown , Co Carlow. John was one of the first people whom I contacted and later in Nov 1996 I sent my written information to Irish TD , Austen Currie.

Figure 2. young girl lying on altar after being drugged NB. This photo was taken from an Irish tabloid highlighting Satanic child abuse But from where did the tabloid reporter the photo?

Devil worshipers plan to sacrifice a baby but to avoid any unwanted attention, they were planning to make one of their own members pregnant and keep the pregnancy secret. The article went on to say that the optimum time for their sacrifice would be the oncoming pagan festival of Halloween. NB.

In my own experiences, at the receiving end of the Satanists attentions, the satanics never leave the abductions of people to the last days unless they are really confident that their "Judas Goat", or the confidant of the victim, can deliver for certain on the day. During the years 1995/6/7 I came under pressure from certain people about 3 weeks before Hallo'een . It was not until 1997 did I realize that these dates were very significant to those who were trying to abduct me. It was quite amazing because for most of the year these same "people" did not

0 secondsThe Burning of Human Bodies to Ashes

show any interest in me. This was a new and extremely strange situation for me, one that I had never experienced before in my lifetime.

NB - I believe that this is an important point for those who read this article. I have no doubt that I can show a definite pattern regarding the dates when Irish people went missing. I will show this pattern in a different article on this site! It would be a very good idea for those who are concerned about satanists, to be very carefull on the run up to Hallo'een and be especially carefull of so-called Christian sects! Controversial book - "Disappeared off the face of the earth"! Irelands most controversial book! Copyright of Jim Cairns Kilkenny Ireland

Chapter 2
The practice of cremation is an heathenic or pagan practice which is an abomination to the God of the righteous

B efore we get into the history of the practice of the children of God in regards to the way they dispose of their dead, let's establish that the practice of cremation is a pagan practice Observe what the scripture says in second kings sixteen verse three. It says: *But he walked in the way of the kings of Israel, yea, and made his son to pass through the fire, according to the abominations of the heathen whom the Lord cast out from before the children of Israel.*

If one is not careful to seriously examine this passage, it is very easy to assume that this practice was that of the kings or ruler-ship of Israel, the people of God. However, a deeper look at the passage reveals that this practice was originated in the lifestyle of the heathen. Note what the Lord God of the children of Israel said regarding where this practice was originated: *according to the abomination of the heathen* . Notice further that those were the people whom the Lord God of Israel cast out from the land prior to placing the children of Is -

rael there. It came straight out of the pagan or hethenic practice

The context of this passage reveals that the kings of Israel have adopted this practice so well that it had become the method or ways of kings in Israel and their people. Notice carefully that by using the word *abominations*, which means a conscious and willful provocation, the Lord not only distanced Himself from ever approving such practice but further, He had a divine disdain for the practice.

God already established the elevation of humanity as being spiritually distinct from all other creatures which He had created. Observe what the scripture says in Geneses one verses twenty-six through twenty-eight: **26** *And God said,* **Let us make man in our image, after our likeness** *and let them* **have dominion over the fish of the sea, and over the fowl of the air, and over the cattle, and over all the earth, and over every creeping thing that creepeth upon the earth.** **27** *So* **God created man in his own image** *in the image of God cre - ated he him* **male and female created he them28** **And God blessed them**, *and* **God said unto them, Be fruitful, and multiply, and replenish the earth, and subdue it:** *and have do minion over the fish of the sea, and over the fowl of the air, and over every living thing that moveth upon the earth.*

The primary distinction of humanity versus any other creature of the Almighty God is that he, that is mankind was made in the image of God Himself. They carry valuable traits of their Creator. They are made after the likeness of God who is their Creator. No other creature has been given such elevated distinction, not one. This is an exclusive with mankind... he carries traits of his very own Creator and as such esteemed with the sanctity of his Creator in life and in death.

Notice further that mankind is given dominion over all the other creatures of God, by God, Himself. This is an authority that is placed on no other creature. This is further expanded into mankind given the sole authority to subdue, yea to conquer and rule over every other creature, not the other way around. Notice further that this sacred authority of man over all the other creatures extends onto them regulatory and managerial powers over the proliferation or procreation of all the other creatures to God's productive end. Notice that he is commanded to not only multiply and replenish the earth but the fact is that no other creature was given that command. This established him, that is mankind, as the ones responsible for the productive end of the proliferation and procreation of all creatures, including themselves. They are the ones who are accountable to God, their Creator for the productive outcome of this process to His honor and glory.

As such, you don't just dispose of mankind like that of the beast or any other creature. There is a level of sanctity that God, the Creator requires of humanity because in handling the life and death of humanity, one needs to be careful to handle such with care because God's image and likeness are wrapped up in him. You may have already deducted that God not only requires of us to handle humanity with sanctity and care but He, Himself does the same. This is why He, that is God, sent His only begotten Son to die for the entire human race.

Chapter 3
The practice of the children of God down through biblical history has always been to bury their dead

Notice first of all that Abraham who is the father of the children of God practiced the burial of his dead. Observe what Genesis twenty-three verses nineteen through twenty say: **19** *And after this, **Abraham buried Sarah his wife** in the cave of the field of Machpelah before Mamre: the same is Hebron in the land of Canaan.* **20** *And **the field, and the cave** that is therein, **were made sure unto Abraham for a possession of a buryingplace by the sons of Heth***

The first factor found in this passage is that Abraham buried his wife. Second, he buried her in a prepared place , appropriately prepared for her burial. The cave was the burial ground which Abraham bought and was designated exclusively for his family's burial. Observe the latter part of verse twenty: "*the field, and the cave   that is therein, **were made sure unto Abraham for a possession of a buryingplace by the sons of Heth.***"

Cremation and the Bible

Abraham paid a pretty penny for that field to secure or pre-
pare a burial ground for his family. Observe what Geneses
forty-nine and verses twenty-nine through thirty-two say:
*"**29** And he charged them, and said unto them, I am to be
gathered unto my people: **bury me with my fathers in the
cave that is in the field of Ephron the Hittite, 30** In the cave
that is in the field of Machpelah, which is before Mamre, in
the land of Canaan, **which Abraham bought with the field of
Ephron the Hittite for a possession of a buryingplace
31 There they buried Abraham and Sarah his wife, there
they buried Isaac and Rebekah his wife;** and **there I buried
Leah 32 The purchase of the field and of the cave that is
therein was from the children of Heth."*

The speaker in this passage was Jacob who was Abraham's
descendant. He was carrying on the practice that his fathers
have started. He charged his sons with no uncertain terms to
see to it that he is placed together with his ancestors. He further charged, also with no uncertain terms that he *"be
buried"* with his fathers in the cave where they were buried.

He further stipulated that he be buried *in the cave that is in
the field of Machpelah, which is before Mamre,* which is the
same field where Abraham buried Sarah. Abraham, himself
was buried. Now Jacob, his discendant was not only stipulat-
ing that he be buried like his fathers but that they buried in
the prepared place which was prepared by his forefather,
Abraham.

He specified further that this field was the one which *Abra
ham bought the field of Ephron the Hittite for a possession
of a buryingplace* Notice that a prepared place along with a
preparation for burial in that specific location was the practice by the father of the children of God which also his seed
followed suit.

From the pages of the scriptures, it is the writer's position that it is accurate to conclude that cremation was not a practice of the children of God but a pagan or hethenic practice It is also safe to conclude that from the scriptures, that the practice of cremation was not a mandate given to the children of God by their God. It is also accurate to conclude that He, that is God has never approved such a practice, neither will he ever. It is not in line with the sanctity of the human makeup and authority placed upon same by his Creator.

What does this say about us preparing a burial place for our family at least for our spouses as men, and if possible, our children? This may not be necessarily in the form of a specific piece of property but in the form of assets. This may also not necessarily be in the form of hard dividends but in the form of an insurance policy that would surely ease the burden of our burial for those left behind and assist them in carrying on after us.

The burring of their dead was an indigenous practice of the nation of Israel. Let us examine the following passage which speaks to that fact. Second Chronicles sixteen verses thirteen through fourteen say: *13. And **Asa slept with his fathers, and died** in the one and fortieth year of his reign. 14. And **they buried him in his own sepulchres, which he had made for himself** in the city of David, and laid him in the bed which was filled with sweet odours and divers kinds of spices **prepared by the apothecaries' {pharmacists} art**: and **they made a very great burning for him**.*

Is this great burning the act of cremation is this the prepa - ration of the spices? Both the scriptural mandates and the culture of the Jewish people who are considered God's chosen people, clearly show what is being referenced here.

The holy oils and ointments were prepared by priests properly qualified for this office. Notice these terms used at the end of verse fourteen in our scripture passage above: *"p.re -*

pared by the apothecaries' {pharmacists} art. " They were qualified to orchestrate the correct combination of fragrances to achieve the required smell. This final result in fragrance would be used to anoint the body to bring a form of dignity to the dead person as they go out from them. This was also a form of honor to the person going out as it was in the case of Mary Magdalene to Jesus *[Matthew 26:12] For in that she hath poured this ointment on my body, she did it for my burial.*

They were also responsible for the preparing of the verity of fragrances used for other occasions, including temple ceremonies. It was God, Himself who commanded Moses to designate the *apothecary pharmacists* as the ones responsible for the carrying out of the mixture of the fragrances. This is confirmed in Exodus thirty verses twenty-two through twenty-five. Observe: *22 Moreover **the LORD spake unto Moses, saying** 23 Take thou also unto thee principal spices, of pure myrrh five hundred shekels, and of sweet cinnamon half so much, even two hundred and fifty shekels, and of sweet calamus two hundred and fifty shekels, 24 And of cassia five hundred shekels, after the shekel of the sanctuary, and of oil olive an hin: 25 And thou shalt make it an **oil of holy ointment**, an **ointment compound after the art of the apothecary** {pharmacists}: it shall be an **holy anointing oil.***

Ecclesiastes chapter ten verse one further confirmed that the fragrances were used to anoint the dead body as a form of preventing decay and to bring dignity to it. Observe: ***Dead flies cause the ointment of the apothecary to send forth a stinking savour:** so doth a little folly him that is in reputation for wisdom and honour.*

The designated duty of the apothecary or pharmacists in the preparing of the fragrances is brought out also in the book of Exodus thirty-seven verse twenty-nine. Observe: *And he made **the holy anointing oil**, and **the pure incense of sweet***

The Burning of Human Bodies to Ashes
spices, according to the work of the apothecary

Notice that they were also responsible for preparing the right mixture of the *holy oil*. As clearly noted in the passage, they were responsible for preparing *the pure incense of sweet spices*. Not only that this specialty of the orchestrating of the fragrances were carried out by a designated set of pharmacists but the practice of the burning of the fragrances for the burial was a perpetual practice by the children of God. This fact is further confirmed in the book Jeremiah thirty-four verses four through five which spoke of *Zedekiah king of Judah* who was indeed a very good king in the sight of the Lord. Observe: *4 Yet hear the word of the LORD, O Zedekiah king of Judah; Thus saith the LORD of thee, Thou shalt not die by the sword: 5 But **thou shalt die in peace:** and **with the burnings of thy fathers, the former kings which were before thee, so shall they burn odours for thee** and **they will lament thee**, saying, Ah lord! for I have pronounced the word, saith the LORD.*

Notice what God said through the prophet Jeremiah regarding the odors that will be burned for King Zedekiah: *"Thou shalt die in peace: and with the burnings for thy fathers, the former kings which were before thee, so shall they burn odours for thee"* Pay even more attention to the reference to the perpetual practice of the dignified burial both for King Zedekiah's forefathers and the former kings before him: *the burnings for thy fathers, the former kings which were before thee.* Notice that the God of the Jews confirmed that this was the practice of not only the former kings but Zedekiah's forefathers.

The absence of this burning of fragrances was highlighted in the book of second Chronicles twenty-one verses eighteen through nineteen as a form of punishment for Jehoram for his way of live being exceptionally evil. Observe: *18 And after all this the LORD smote him in his bowels with an incurable * * disease. 19 And it came to pass, that in process of time,* *after * the end of two years, his bowels fell out by reason of his sickness: so he died of sore diseases. And **his people made no burning for him, like the burning of his fathers***

Note that this withholding of the burning of the fragrances was done by the people and not as a command from the Lord. Notice also that it is confirmed again here that this burning of fragrances at the burial was the practice or their forefathers.

Chapter 4
The preparing of multiple forms of spices at burial by the Jewish people seems to be a practice which continued even into the new testament era.

Observe what the book of Matthew chanter twenty-six verse twelve says: *For in that she hath poured this ointment on my body,* **she did it for my burial.** Here we see the Lord Jesus Christ, speaking of His own burial, embraced the practice of applying the precious fragrances at the burial of a human being. In so doing, He authenticated the practice of the burial of the dead as the acceptable form of disposing the body of a human being.

He, that is Jesus Christ is the perfect example. Here he made reference to His own remedy for the disposal of His own body as with a burial. Even if there were no other reason but the example of Christ our Savior, that would be reason enough for the believers to follow suit and bury their dead.

There is no room for any inferencing from this that you can bury the cremated body. It is clear that one would not anoint the ashes, they would anoint a body. The using of the fragrances to anoint the dead is futile with the body burned to ashes The scripture reference in Ecclesiastes ten and verse one further rules out the notion of using the oils to anoint the ashes. Observe: *Dead flies cause the ointment of the apothecary to send forth a stinking savour: so doth a little folly him that is in reputation for wisdom and honour. bodies whole*

In the first place, there is no bacteria left in the asses to attract flies. Secondly, one of the purposes of preparing the ashes is to prevent decaying. As such, there would be no room for any stinking smell to be included. Thirdly, it is the writer's belief that the reference to dead flies could also be a reference to the maggot which emanates from the body which results from decay.

Far beyond just Jesus speaking in future tense about His body being prepared for burialnstead of being cremated, the scrip - ture records the actual occurrence of this reference. The apostle John wrote in the book of John chapter nineteen verses thirty-nine through forty the following: *39. And there came also **Nicodemus** which at the first came to Jesus by night, and **brought a mixture of myrrh and aloes**, about an hundred pound weight. 40. Then **took they the body** of Jesus and **wound it in linen clothes with the spices, as the manner of the Jews is to bury.***

Notice that *they took the body* instead of the cremated remains. They followed that up by *wrapping the body up in linen clothes.* They also brought with them a collection of fragrances, more specifically myrrh and aloes, "which drugs were used to preserve bodies from putrefaction. Calmet says that the aloes mentioned here is a liquor which runs from an aromatic tree, and is widely different from that called aloes among us." *Adam Clarke Commentary* – The final affirma - tion that the act of burying their dead was the manner or practice of the people of God is found in the latter part of the

The Burning of Human Bodies to Ashes
passage: *as the manner of the Jews is to bury*

According to Matthew's account of this occasion, Joseph is mentioned as also taking Jesus' body and carrying out the same process. Observe his record in Matthew twenty-seven verses fifty-nine through sixty: *59. And when **Joseph had taken the body**, he **wrapped it in a clean linen cloth** , 60. And **laid it in his own new tomb** which he had **hewn out in the rock**: and he rolled a great stone to the door of the sepulchre, and departed.*

This serves not as a contradiction or conflict but a confirmation. If you examine John's account carefully, you will see the following: *"Then **took they the body** f Jesus."* The plural pronoun *'they'* confirms the fact that this was a collective effort. It was both Nicodemus and Joseph who took responsibility for the body of Jesus and made sure that he received a proper burial. Notice further that Matthew confirmed that the body of Jesus was not only taken and prepared for burial but was actually buried in a prepared tomb carved out in the rock.

Chapter 5
The method of the burial of the dead is a physical practice that has a spiritual representation.

The burial of the dead is wrapped up in the spiritual triune parts of the Gospel. The Gospel is the death burial and resurrection of Jesus Christ. The absence of any one portion of those triune functions would mean that we have an incomplete Gospel which would ultimately mean that salvation plan is incomplete. So, then the Gospel is hinged on the burial of the dead body and the resurrection of Jesus Christ.

Observe what the apostle Paul said in first Corinthians fifteen verses one through four: *1. Moreover, brethren, **I declare unto you the gospel** which I preached unto you, which also ye have received, and wherein ye stand; 2. **By which also ye are saved** if ye keep in memory what I preached unto you, unless ye have believed in vain. 3. For I delivered unto you first of all that which I also received, how that **Christ died for our sins according to the scriptures; 4. And that he was buried and that he rose again the third day according to the scriptures:***

28

So, for believers, their dead body undergoing the other two parts of the process to complete the picture of the representation of the Gospel is a matter of spiritual significance. Notice that the apostle Paul said that we were saved by the body of Christ experiencing the three processes of the Gospel: the death, the burial and the resurrection. For Christians to surrender their body to these triune processes is keeping intact the complete picture of the Gospel by which we are saved.

For believers, the practice of burring the dead hinges on the representation of the new life that we have in Christ Jesus. Observe what the apostle Paul wrote in Romans six verses three through four: *3. Know ye not, that **so many of us as were baptized into Jesus Christ** were baptized into his death* *4. Therefore **we are buried with him by baptism into death**: that **like as Christ was raised up from the dead by the glory of the Father, even so we also should walk in newness of life***

For Christians, even separate from the fact that the burial of their dead is an old and new testament practice of the children of God, salvation plan and the new life in Christ is hinged on this triple processes. For Christ, if He did not experience the death on the cross, then sin's death would not have been paid. If He were not buried, then our sins could not be buried with Him in His death. Finally, if He were not risen from the dead then we could not experience the newness of life in Christ.

Even so if we as believers divert from the pattern of burying our dead, we deviate from keeping the complete picture of the Gospel and the new life in Christ intact. Just out of following the Supreme example of our Lord and Savior, Jesus Christ, we should see it necessary to bury our dead. However, baring that factor, we have the process of the Gospel to commemorate by burying our dead whole. We also have the fact that we are experiencing this newness of life to commemorate by burying our dead whole.

Even God, from the very beginning declared that the dead
body should return to the ground from which it came. Ob
serve His words in Geneses three verse nineteen: *In the sweat
of thy face shalt thou eat bread, **till thou return unto the
ground** for **out of it wast thou taken** : for **dust thou art,** and
unto dust shalt thou return.*

This passage resonates that mankind's life consists of labor-
ing by the sweat of his face and reaping his labor by eating
bread. It also resonates that mankind's destiny is to return to
the ground because out of it he came. The passage went on
to resonate that the body is dust and unto the dust shall it return.

The writer of the book of Ecclesiastes reiterated this same
predicament for mankind. Observe what he wrote in Ecclesiastes twelve verses five through seven: *5. Also when they
shall be afraid of that which is high, and fears shall be in the
way, and the almond tree shall flourish, and the grasshopper
shall be a burden, and desire shall fail: **because man goeth
to his long home** and the **mourners go about the streets**: 6.
Or ever the silver cord be loosed, or the golden bowl be broken, or the pitcher be broken at the fountain, or the wheel
broken at the cistern. 7. **Then shall the dust return to the
earth as it was**: and the spirit shall return unto God who gave
it.*

If nothing else convinces us that the burial of our dead is a
theocratic principle and biblical mandate, then we should surrender to the example of God, Himself performing this same
method of disposing the dead body of the human.

Observe what God did with the body of Moses in the book of
Deuteronomy chapter thirty-four verses five through six: *5.
So **Moses the servant of the LORD died** there in the land of*

The Burning of Human Bodies to Ashes

*Moab, according to the word of the LORD. 6. And **he buried him in a valley in the land of Moab**, over against Bethpeor: but no man knoweth of his sepulchre unto this day.*

Note that *Moses the servant of the LORD died in the land of Moab.* Notice further that He, who is the Lord, buried him in the valley of the land of Moab. If God, the Creator of mankind utilized the method of burying the body as a means of disposing of the human body, what other example do we need?

Our Lord and Savior, Jesus Christ placed His approval on the method of the burial of the dead bodies as an acceptable method to Him. In the book of Matthew chapter eight verse twenty-two we find the following words of Jesus: *But Jesus said unto him, Follow me; and **let the dead bury their dead**.* What Jesus was saying here is to let the spiritually dead which is the unsaved, bury the physically dead but those whom He called should follow Him. By saying *let the dead bury their dead,* Jesus authenticated the process of the burial of the dead as the acceptable method of disposing the dead human body instead of any other means, including cremation.

Index

A

a buryingplace 19, 20
abomination 16
abominations 12, 16, 17
abominations of the heathen 16
Abraham buried his wife 19
Abraham buried Sarah his wife 19
Abraham to offer up his son Isaac 11
accountable to God 18

B

biblical standards 8, 12
burial 5, 19, 20, 21, 22, 23, 24, 25, 26, 27, 28, 29, 30, 31
buried her in a prepared place 19
buried him in his own sepulchres 21
buried in the cave 20
buried in the prepared place 20
buried with him by baptism 29
buried with Him in His death 29
buried" with his fathers 20
burn odours for thee 23
burn their sons and their daughters in the fire 12
burned the bones into lime 9
burned the bones of the king 9, 12
burned to ashes 10, 12, 26
burning the bones of the human carcass 10
burnt his bones 9
burnt the bones 9
burring the dead hinges on the representation of the new life 29
bury me with my fathers 20

C

child as a sacrifice 12
child sacrifice 12 13
complete picture of the Gospel 29
consumed by the fire 12
Cremation 3, 4, 5, 6, 7, 8, 9, 10, 12, 14, 16, 18, 20, 21, 22, 24, 26, 28, 30, 31

W